THE 'Q' TRADITION

T0345970

THE 'Q' TRADITION

An Inaugural Lecture

By

BASIL WILLEY

Fellow of Pembroke College
King Edward VII Professor of English Literature
in the University of Cambridge

CAMBRIDGE
At the University Press

1946

CAMBRIDGE
UNIVERSITY PRESS

University Printing House, Cambridge CB2 8BS, United Kingdom

Published in the United States of America by Cambridge University Press, New York

Cambridge University Press is part of the University of Cambridge.

It furthers the University's mission by disseminating knowledge in the pursuit of
education, learning and research at the highest international levels of excellence.

www.cambridge.org
Information on this title: www.cambridge.org/9781107688605

© Cambridge University Press 1946

First published 1946
Re-issued 2014

A catalogue record for this publication is available from the British Library

ISBN 978-1-107-68860-5 Paperback

THE 'Q' TRADITION

THOUGH I have now had some months in which to contemplate my new (and to me very formidable) responsibilities, I have not yet recovered from the shock of surprise with which I first found myself, in the words of a friendly colleague in another Faculty, '*encouched* in Arthur's Seat'. The King Edward VII Chair is indeed Arthur's Seat by double prescriptive right, for its only two previous occupants have been Arthur Verrall and Arthur Quiller-Couch. Verrall was a sick man when he was appointed, and lived only to complete one course of lectures; his fine and brilliant intellect has thus left little mark upon the English School. It is with 'Q' that the Chair will long continue to be associated in the minds of all who knew and loved him, and of us, especially, who felt his influence; much longer, that is, than the wise and merciful statutes now in force will permit me to wear his mantle. 'Q's' rich personality, his wisdom and wit, and his inimitable gusto, lent an almost legendary glamour to the Chair he held so long, and a daunting sense of unworthiness must needs oppress the heart of his successor. We shall not look upon his like again. Encouragement to face the task of continuing his work, however, has come first from the generous goodwill of many colleagues and friends, and also from the hope that, as one of 'Q's' disciples, I might perhaps do something to preserve the spirit of his teaching.

> That I am favour'd for unworthiness,
> By such propitious parley medicin'd
> In sickness not ignoble, I rejoice,
> Aye, and could weep for love of such award.

'Q', in his Inaugural Lecture, gracefully impersonating Plato's Athenian Stranger, lamented that Cambridge, though it had feasted him and cast a gown over him, could not furnish him with precedents and traditions such as other Professors enjoyed. The Chair was 'a new one, or almost new', and, as he said, it seemed to float in the void, like Mahomet's coffin. We may recall that in 1913 there was still no English Tripos; Verrall for the whole of his brief tenure, and 'Q' for the first four years of his, had no autonomous English School to address.

Amongst the innumerable advantages 'Q' had over me, that of assuming office as a ξένος must be counted an important if minor one (not that, like Dryden in that poet's last and blackest apostasy, 'Q' ever implied that Cambridge was Thebes to Oxford's Athens). To me is allotted the extra handicap of having to try and be a prophet in my own country. However, one great advantage I do enjoy: there has now been an English School and an English Tripos here for nearly thirty years, and I have behind me a precedent and a tradition, those of 'Q' himself. The precedent I cannot hope to emulate, but the tradition I do hope in some small measure to continue, or at least to adapt (as all living traditions must be adapted) to the changed and changing conditions of our time. For the 'Q' tradition does live on vigorously here, and the Cambridge English School owes to this, I believe, most of what distinguishes it (to its advantage, in my view) from the corresponding Schools elsewhere. 'Others will carry it on,' wrote 'Q' in the Preface to *The Art of Writing* (referring to his own work here), 'though my effort come to naught.' It has not come to naught, and it is my hope that it never will. This particular moment of history—when the tyranny of war is over-

past, and when lecturers again have to face, like 'Q'
in 1919, an audience strengthened by many ex-
warriors who will stand no nonsense—affords a good
opportunity for taking stock of our tradition and
interrogating the future. Let us ask first, then, what
is this 'Q' tradition, and for what special values has
his English School here so far stood?

The time is now past, I think, when it could be
seriously doubted whether English would ever provide a respectable academic discipline. Some hint of
the state of opinion thirty-six years ago may be derived
from the playful remarks of the *Cambridge Review*,
addressed to the Prime Minister in October 1912,
during the short interregnum between Verrall and
'Q':

> Perhaps the Prime Minister will not resent the reminder
> that we are still without a King Edward VII Professor of
> English Literature....We know that there are other
> matters to occupy Mr Asquith's attention, and the
> University has indeed managed to make shift for some
> centuries without a Professor of English Literature. Still
> this is the era of the *Daily Mail*, and a Professor is surely
> needed.

On that last point 'Q' would have agreed with me
in commenting, 'je n'en vois pas la nécessité'. But

on the need for a University School of English Literature 'Q' never wavered, and still less should we waver now. He knew, and proclaimed, that the Universities were not founded for the study of any literature, least of all our own, and only 'tardily admitted it'. 'Greek in 1540', as he said, 'Latin not until 1869, English but three years ago—from the lesson of these intervals there is no getting away.' But the justification he offered for such studies has become even more weighty than it was thirty years ago. There should be a University School, he held, where youth is trained in two main disciplines: the Art of Reading, and the Art of Writing. Let us consider each of these in turn.

We may usefully remind ourselves, first, of the expressed intention of the founder of this Chair: 'The Professor', it is enacted, 'shall treat this subject on literary and critical rather than on philological and linguistic lines'—and here I would humbly apply to myself 'Q's' comment: 'a proviso which at any rate cuts off a cantle of the new Professor's ignorance.' It is this proviso, chiming in so perfectly with 'Q's' own temper and convictions, which has chiefly determined the lines along which English studies at Cambridge have proceeded. From the outset 'Q' insisted that Literature must be studied for its own sake, as a living art, and not for the sake of acquiring accessory information about it, useful and important though those accessories might be. This meant that the first part of the discipline must be training in the art of reading, which further implies the cultivation of critical judgement, or the power to appraise and evaluate literary works. To those who thought English was a 'soft option', or a dilettante 'meandering amongst books', he replied in effect that the grappling with masterpieces, with intent to discover their total meaning and value, is one of the most difficult tasks the human mind can be set to accomplish. 'That task', as he said, 'and nothing less difficult, will always be the one worthiest of a great University.' We must wean ourselves from 'Germanic' standards, leaving the shady wood where pedantic bats and owls flutter in search of origins, sources, influences and tendencies, and expose ourselves to the glorious light of literature itself. His point always was, not that true scholarship is to be despised—'I worship great learning', he once said—but that even scholarship, and of course *a fortiori* pedantry, is only valuable as preparation for the essential, the far more exacting experience, that of fully and critically apprehending the finished product, the work of literary art. One is reminded of the seventeenth-century distinction between religion itself and the 'things about religion', or of Thomas à Kempis' remark, beloved of 'Q', that it is better to feel compunction than to know its definition. The 'things about literature' are, many of them, fascinating and worth knowing, but they are easily learnt; the widening and refining of our critical sensibility, this is the real thing, *hic labor, hoc opus est*. It is this that calls the whole soul of man into activity, with subordination of the faculties each to each according to their several worth and dignity; it is to the attainment of this discriminating judgement, this instinctive sense of value, that all education in humane letters, whether classical or vernacular, should lead. I would go further, and say that all education which neglects this aim is woefully incomplete, that much that now passes for education is actually incomplete, and that our modern world is dangerously ill in consequence of this very defect. 'Q' once illustrated the difficulty of this critical training, as compared with learning about literature, by remarking that 'no one can have set a General Paper on Literature and examined on it, setting it and marking the answers, alongside of papers about language, inflexions and the rest', without realizing that it is in dealing critically with a book or play that the candidate generally flounders, whereas in the other matters 'a pupil with a moderately retentive memory will easily obtain sixty or seventy per cent of the total marks'. We have learnt a good deal since 'Q's' early lectures, both from him and still more from others, about this art of reading, and nothing that we have learnt makes it seem any easier or less worthy of attainment. Indeed, there is much evidence to suggest that it ought to be the true end of liberal education, the end to which all other studies should be means. I say 'ought' and 'should be', for we all know how disastrously our modern world falls short of this ideal, and how perilously near we have come to losing our sense of direction, and our hold upon what ultimately matters most. 'Q' took great pains to explode this myth of the easiness of literary study, and I hope and believe that I am preaching to the already converted; yet myths die hard, and I suspect that this one may still occasionally haunt us, like that other which erroneously avers that life in Jesus and Pembroke Colleges is all play and no work. Easy? To produce, from the raw material of youth, men and women of genuine culture, full of wisdom and understanding, rich natures furnished with ability, sure in judgement, able to distinguish the best from the second-best, the genuine from the counterfeit, striving constantly towards the good life? All this is *easy*? Visionary, if you like, impracticable, idealistic, but not *easy*. Yet these are the aims of the English School. Indeed, if we ever stopped to ask ourselves the question, we should say that they are the aims of all true education, and the aims, above all, of University Education. I make bold to claim that the Cambridge English School, which has always stood for these values, has a special responsibility at this present time to defend them against odds, and perhaps even a special opportunity to become their principal champion—or shall we say, one of their two or three champions. For at this point, without entering upon controversy, I want to offer humble and deferential acknowledgements to our Classical friends, whose School has so long and so illustriously been in the vanguard. Long may 'Classics' keep its honourable place in the front of the battle! We will follow, proud to be second to such a senior. For as I see it, our aims are theirs, and theirs ours, so far as both are worthy of themselves.

In so far as 'Classics' remembers its own essential idea, it must be striving to produce just such results as we, and perhaps with better chance of success. In so far as 'English' is true to its aim, it must keep in touch with classical antiquity, and must cultivate those habits of clear and precise thought, that exactness in interpretation, which 'Classics' has fostered through study of ancient texts. I would never, for my part, wish anyone to embark upon the study of English at Cambridge without a thorough previous grounding in Classics; neither, I am sure, would the Classical School be satisfied if its pupils failed to turn their advantages to still more glorious gain by pressing on into the literature of their mother-tongue. But, as I see it, the prospect actually is (and I view it with dismay) that the Universities will soon be thronged with young people knowing no Latin and no Greek (and perhaps ignorant of the Bible as well), yet seeking for what we can give them of genuine culture. What shall we do for such? It may be that 'English' will have to assume responsibility for them, and try to do for them, through English Literature, something of what Classics has done in the past through Greek and Latin. If it prove so, let our Classical allies think no evil of us! I would plead for their sympathetic support, and ask them to think of us as their offspring, compelled by malign necessity to fight their battle lacking some of their weapons, and in territory where they can give us little direct aid. Perhaps, when the great Philistine is beyond the reach of the main army of Israel, our pebble may find its mark. This (by the way), like many similar allusions (so we shall inform our raw multitudes), comes from a famous classic which used in former times to have much influence on men's thoughts and practices, and we shall advise them to read it. And in like manner we may be able to send some repentant prodigals back to their Greek and Latin fathers when they have discovered, by studying Spenser, Milton, Pope and some others, how little they know of English who only English know.

Yet, while bating not a jot of what I have just said, let me try to be 'indifferent honest'; let me not dissemble nor cloak my real thoughts, but freely acknowledge and confess that I was in earnest when I suggested that 'English' might now have a special duty and opportunity to uphold the standards of humane culture in these dark latter days. I do not wish to pitch our claims too low, so let me say that I think we are furnished with better weapons, in our fight with Goliath, than what Sir T. Browne called 'contemptible pibbles' drawn from the 'scrip and slender stock' of ourselves. Others have sung the glories of our blood and state, and it is not needful for me or anyone else now to demonstrate that our native dramatists, poets, philosophers or historians are excellent substitutes for those of antiquity (though ideally we should be familiar with both); or that there are English texts obscure enough to sharpen the wits of the young almost as effectively as the dead languages did. I was thinking rather of the position of culture amidst the spiritual anarchy of to-day, an anarchy so much more sinister than that which disturbed Arnold in 1867. First, there is the spectre of over-specialization, of which we hear so much to-day. Culture, as Matthew Arnold said, aims at the 'full perfection of our humanity', but we seem to be thinking more now of its full destruction, first by training people as specialized technicians, and then by using their results to abolish mankind altogether. It almost looks as if the Eden of Genesis prefigured this great globe itself, and that the apple forbidden to man was the atomic bomb which may blow him right out of the planet. We have forgotten Bacon's warning, uttered at the very outset of our modern Faustian era, that what saves knowledge from the serpent is Charity—that it shall be directed to the glory of God and the relief of man's estate. This is still the defence of literary culture in our time, as it was in Arnold's, that by learning and propagating the best that has been thought and said in the world, it may help to make reason and the will of God prevail. In an age when nations, classes and individuals are all snatching madly after economic or political advantage, and misusing science to serve such ends, Culture may remind us that we are still men, and that goodness and mercy might follow us all our days if only we would cultivate the fruits of the spirit instead of the Satanic apples which turn to bombs as we pluck them. On all this, 'Q', speaking in the middle of the first world war, has some remarks which are still more pertinent now. After referring to Browning's division of the soul into What Is, What Knows and What Does, with Being at the summit, and Knowledge and Action in descending order below, he breaks out:

. . . does it not strike you how curiously men to-day, with their minds perverted by hate, are inverting that order?—All the highest value set on *What Does*—*What Knows* suddenly seen to be of importance, but only as important in feeding the guns, perfecting explosives, collaring trade —all in the service of 'Efficiency'; no one stopping to think that 'Efficiency' is a relative term! Efficient for what?—for *What Does, What Knows* or perchance, after all, for *What Is*? No! banish the humanities and throw everybody into practical science: not into that study of natural science, which can never conflict with the 'humanities' since it seeks discovery for the pure sake of truth, or charitably to alleviate man's lot...but to invent what will be commercially serviceable in besting your neighbour, or in gassing him, or in slaughtering him neatly and wholesale. (*Art of Reading*, pp. 8–9.)

How much, if anything, can Culture, aiming at 'the full perfection of our humanity', do to arrest this frantic rush down a steep place into the sea? Arnold himself was not over sanguine: it may, he said, stem 'the common tide of men's thoughts in a wealthy and industrial community', and may 'save the future...from being vulgarized, even if it cannot save the present.' Alas! we have more than vulgarization to fear—though heaven knows we have that too, and in forms that would have driven Arnold to despair. Moreover, Arnold believed that the highest form of Culture was religion. The highest art, he said, in one of the *American Discourses*, 'is an art which by its height, depth and gravity possesses religiousness'; and conversely, religion must pass into poetry if it is to penetrate and transform 'that poor inattentive and immoral creature, man'. On this vital issue I do not think it my province to speak, but I give you my private opinion that mere literary culture, unless in some sense it 'possesses religiousness', has the use of its left hand only. However, many to-day are left-handed, and the left hand can do something, even much. If literature is, in Shelley's phrase, 'the record of the best and happiest moments of the happiest and best minds', or in the phrase of a former colleague here, 'the storehouse of recorded values', then the more people we can induce to decipher that record and frequent that storehouse the better. Perhaps some of these in doing so will be driven back, not only upon the classical sources of our literature as I have suggested, but also upon the religious foundations on which those excellent moments, and those recorded values, ultimately rested. But here I return to my point: it seems probable that henceforth more and more young people, if they are to share the moments and accept the values, will have to find them in the storehouse of *English* literature, or not at all.

This, then, is the chief *raison d'être* of an English

School in a University to-day. I would add, before leaving the subject of over-specialization, that literary study, properly conducted as a discipline, is an admirable corrective to that dangerous tendency. It is a corrective because it encourages the free play of mind and sensibility over the whole range of human life—for the subject-matter of literature is nothing less than this. 'Q' used to mock at the expression 'the subject of English Literature'—'And I never even knew that English Literature had a "subject"; or rather supposed it to have several!' Hear him also on the specialist, the man who wants to know everything about something:

> You produce [he said] a brain bulging out inordinately on one side, on the other cut flat down and mostly paralytic at that: and in short so long as I hold that the Creator has an idea of a man, so long shall I be sure that no uneven specialist realizes it. (*Art of Reading*, p. 13.)

An English School like ours tries, on the other hand, not to distend one lobe of the brain, but to develop complete human beings, to call the *whole* soul into activity, feeling, imagination, judgement, taste and intelligence as well as memory. A literary training can produce just that flexibility of mind, that detachment and poise, of which we stand so gravely in need.

A man cannot be steeped in literature, cannot have formed some standards of criticism, without having used all the faculties of the soul—intelligence and memory to learn, sympathetic imagination to interpret the thought and utterance of men in differing ages and situations, and wisdom to discern the enduring human needs and imperatives beneath the changing surfaces. It is just this unspecialized wisdom that the world cries out for now, and it is just this that the study of literature can best hope to foster. Here again we find that 'Q' has said the appropriate word:

> The man we are proud to send forth from our Schools will be remarkable less for something he can take out of his wallet and exhibit as knowledge, than for being something, and that something recognizable for a man of unmistakable intellectual breeding, whose trained judgement we can trust to choose the better and reject the worse. (Inaugural Lecture, *Art of Writing*, p. 12.)

It is because I believe this to be the true function of an English School that I am glad our own has maintained the 'Q' tradition, and, concerning itself mainly with literature and criticism, has not made philology compulsory. The founder of this Chair was perhaps wiser than he knew when he introduced that above-quoted proviso; he was prescribing the function of the Chair, of course, not that of the School itself, but in so doing he made possible the appointment of 'Q', and the rest has followed. Now I mean no disrespect to philology in saying this; as 'Q' himself remarked, 'there is no surer sign of intellectual ill-breeding than to speak, even to feel, slightingly of any knowledge one does not happen to possess'. I am glad that philology (or the history of the language beginning with Anglo-Saxon) is not compulsory in the English Tripos, just as I am glad that scholastic philosophy or economic history are not compulsory, although these subjects may have a greater bearing on modern literature than Anglo-Saxon has. They are all great subjects, but they are different subjects, and a student who is seriously undergoing our special discipline will find two or three years too short a time in which to become all that we expect of him. I should add that I strongly approve of the present inclusion of Anglo-Saxon and the History of the Language as optional papers in our Tripos; there are some minds to whom this approach is congenial, and their needs should be provided for. It is true that the Cambridge English School stands almost alone in this respect, but it has had, and I hope will continue to have, its own distinctive witness, and should continue along its own line without faltering. In these days of stereotyping and central planning it is temptingly easy to fall into line, and dress by the right (or perhaps rather by the left). Universities, above all, should resist any attempts to turn them into Uniformities, and if our English School is different from others, that should be a reason for keeping it so, as long as it is realizing its own idea.

But I have not yet stated the whole of what I take that 'idea' to be, and I want now briefly to sketch the rest of it. In doing so I hope also to be replying, in effect, to certain probable criticisms of the School. What follows is not, I think, an abandonment of my previous positions, though at first it may have that appearance.

Someone may say: 'All this talk about Culture and human values may be very fine and large, but isn't your aim too narrowly aesthetic? Aren't you in danger, by cutting yourself adrift from all the traditional disciplines, of getting caught up in the whirligig of taste? Will your finished product, the man you are proud to send forth, be really, as you say, a man of unmistakable intellectual breeding? Is he not more likely to be a coxcomb in whom you have raised "a treasonable growth of indecisive judgements", and will he not vent these upon the world with all the pert assurance of immaturity? Have you no stiffening discipline to offer?'

Well, as to most of all this, it is perhaps enough to reply that man is a fallen creature, prone to err, a creature whose 'erected wit' (in Sidney's words) 'maketh us know what perfection is', but whose 'infected will keepeth us from reaching unto it'. You can attack any good institution or any ideal—Christianity, democracy, the Classical Tripos, or what you will—by pointing out that its adherents often fail to live up to its standards. I doubt if the English School is more open to criticism on this score than any other. But the points about narrow aestheticism and stiffening discipline admit of a more precise rejoinder.

First, I would insist that the 'Q' tradition set itself from the start against any narrowly aesthetic approach. Literature must be studied for its own sake—yes, but what is Literature? With what does it deal? Literature may be roughly described as what has been memorably written about human life, by persons of unusual sensibility and intellectual power.

I know this is too loose a formula; moreover, much that is read in other schools is also literature, and much that we must read in ours is not. My point is that the subject-matter of literature is Life, and it was against the divorce of literature from life that 'Q' contended most vehemently. It was the reduction of literature to an abstract 'subject', or science, a dead carcass for pedants to peck at, that he most detested. A writer in *The Times* ten years ago put the matter well:

A man of letters without pedantry, the least academic professor that ever found his lectures thronged as great public entertainments, he has been determined...that, just where literature is most in danger of becoming a 'subject' and losing touch with life, there it should be most resolutely held out in the daylight, to be seen as a natural function of man. In that conviction all his own writing has been done.

I think that to 'Q' this chiefly meant the personal approach to books, regarding them, that is to say, as the work of men and women who have toiled and wept and loved and laughed and prayed, people at all points like ourselves, but endowed with the gift of memorable speech. It meant what Milton meant when he said that 'a good book is the precious life-blood of a master spirit, embalmed and treasured upon purpose to a life beyond life'—a view of literature akin to Carlyle's view of history as the biographies of great men. It may be felt, however, that this connection between literature and life is a matter that needs closer and more exact examination, that here, in fact, is a point where the 'Q' tradition needs adapting to our expanded knowledge. 'Literature is a natural function of man'—but the meaning of this phrase has been greatly enriched in recent times by the later developments in psychology, sociology, economics and the like. We are accustomed now to connect literature with life, not so much by linking books with their authors, as by viewing them in their historical setting, and in relation to their social or intellectual (may I use the horrid word?) 'background'. Literary movements, it is realized, cannot fully be explained without reference to forces at work outside the field of literature itself; the way men write is conditioned by the way they live and work and think and feel. Sticking to our position that literature must not be divorced from life, we thus find ourselves compelled to study history as well, especially social and economic history, and the history of religious, moral and political ideas. And is this narrow aestheticism? Are we so wanting in stiffening discipline? Alas! what we need is not more discipline, but more time—or at least some discrimination, to teach us where to draw the line. But in fact some sort of line has always been drawn, and this study of backgrounds is no new thing. The Tripos has always been the English Tripos, not the English Literature Tripos, and Literature has always been linked in the rubrics with Life and Thought. 'Q', here as ever our prophet and tutelary spirit, laid down the following as the first of our governing tenets:

That literature cannot be divorced from life: that (for example) you cannot understand Chaucer aright, unless you have the background, unless you know the kind of men for whom Chaucer wrote and the kind of men whom he made speak. (*Art of Reading*, p. 114.)

And it is to 'Q' that we owe the introduction of the paper on the English Moralists in Part II—the most important, in my (perhaps prejudiced) view, of the later developments in our syllabus. Nevertheless, I do not pretend that we manage these linkages as well as we might. Life and thought (except perhaps in the mediaeval period) are not studied enough, and not brought into proper relation with literature. It is here that there is most room for reform, and if we are to modify the Tripos in the coming years, it is in the direction of a closer alliance with History and the Moral Sciences that I think we should move. In what I have previously said I may have seemed to imply that English alone could provide a complete training in the humanities; why, it might be asked, if we are to believe you, should any Arts student read anything else? Of course that was not what I meant. This is not the occasion to outline any possible Cambridge Modern Greats, but let me repeat that a closer interchange between 'English' and 'History' in particular is what I should like to see. History, as Aristotle remarked, deals with what has happened, with events, with the particular; poetry, with what might happen, with the universal. He even said that poetry was a higher and more philosophical thing than history for that reason. I make no such boast, though when, as an undergraduate, after transferring from History to English, I first met with the phrase, I admit that it comforted me. History deals with past events; literature, let us say, deals in part with men's feelings about events. We shall never understand the feelings unless we are familiar with the events. Here let me invoke the wisdom of Professor

Trevelyan (if he will allow me to quote a few phrases he has lately written):

'Literature and history are twin sisters, inseparable.' 'Unless our great English literature is to become a sealed book to the English people (as indeed I fear it is to many), our countrymen must know something of times past.'

History, he concludes, 'is not the rival of Classics or of modern literature, or of the political sciences. It is rather the house in which they all dwell. It is the cement that holds together all the studies relating to the nature and achievements of man.' Very well! And since we cannot all live in the great house, let us borrow some of the builder's cement to reinforce our prefabricated hut. Literature communicates men's feelings, I have said, and that means that we must learn what Psychology can teach about the workings of human nature, both individually and socially. It also communicates men's thoughts, so we must look to Philosophy to train us in habits of exact reasoning. It communicates their highest yearnings after the chief Good, so we must understand the religion from which our civilization has sprung. Moreover, to understand our own literature aright, we should know something of at least one, if not more, of the modern European literatures. Our present perfunctory glances at French and Italian in Part II seem to me inadequate, and I should like to see the study of comparative literature taken more seriously. We may be over-ambitious, but 'narrowly aesthetic'?—no, not that.

I conclude with a few remarks about that other discipline which was so close to 'Q's' heart: the study of the Art of Writing. He never tired of insisting that 'as Literature is an Art and therefore not to be pondered only, but practised, so ours is a living language, and therefore to be kept alive, supple, and active in all honourable use'. 'If', he wrote, 'with all our native exemplars to give us courage, we persist in striving to write well, we can easily resign to other nations the secondary fame to be picked up by commentators.' This is probably the most familiar aspect of the 'Q' tradition—his lecture on Jargon has become a classic—but surely we need to remind ourselves of it more than ever to-day. In his second lecture he thus addressed his audience:

Yes, I seriously propose to you that here in Cambridge we *practise writing*: that we practise it not only for our own improvement, but to make, or at least try to make, appropriate, perspicuous, accurate, persuasive writing a recognizable hall-mark of anything turned out by our English School.

Alas! If only it were so! I fear that what 'Q' said in 1913 is truer still to-day:

Jargon stalks unchecked in our midst. It is becoming the language of Parliament: it has become the medium through which Boards of Government, County Councils, Syndicates, Committees, Commercial Firms, express the processes as well as the conclusions of their thought and so voice the reason of their being.

Truer still, for we must add to this list the Cinema, the radio, the new scientific jargons, and other influences less easily named, which press upon us now on all sides. One would like to think that here in Cambridge, in 'Q's' English School, the well of English was kept pure and undefiled. But it is the sad experience of all supervisors that even of those whose love of literature leads them here, and who may be supposed to have begun their literary training at school and at home, very few indeed show any sense of English style, any instinct for appropriate, accurate, perspicuous, let alone persuasive or euphonious, writing. The scientists—all honour to them!— are becoming alarmed at the illiteracy of their pupils, and are looking to us for help. This should put us on our mettle; we must minister to the Jews first, before we can carry salvation to the Gentiles. I am afraid the causes of all this lie deep in our social and spiritual condition; the malady is constitutional, and cannot be cured by surface remedies. Style, like religion, and the moral virtues, is caught rather than taught; if we lack style, it is because we are suffering from some spiritual blight, some coarsening of the fibre, some vulgarization of the sensibility, some obscuration of fixed standards and clear aims. If it is harder than ever to-day to write well, that is because it is harder than ever to live, feel and think well. We are not even agreed upon the question of what is or is not good style; some styles, formerly thought good, are now considered pompous, or em-purpled, or precious, or indicative of some obsolete phase in the class struggle. One thing seems clear: since style is the index of the man and his environ-ment, and not a cosmetic applied from outside, the good style must always be that which genuinely expresses him and his predicament. If it is genuine, his style may be a poor thing as compared with those of happier men in happier ages, but it will be at least his own. It is useless to try to acquire style by aping the manners of the past; of all styles the bogus-literary is least desirable. We do not censure William Walton because his music is so unlike Mendelssohn's, or Mr Eliot because he does not write like Tennyson or Robert Bridges. The whole tempo and texture of human life have changed so profoundly since the nineteenth century—even since 'Q' took office—that good prose can no longer be written in the manner of Ruskin or Pater, or even of 'Q' himself. To attempt this is to commit the sin of Waterhouse. This means that good prose style to-day, like good modern architecture, will probably be 'functional', bare, hard, lacking in grace and tenderness, but at least clean and firm; or, like much modern music and verse, it may be rapid, glancing, elliptical, assuming much that would formerly have been stated at length. Its vocabulary will inevitably contain many scientific terms, and probably some Americanisms. 'Q' wrote so well, because in everything that he wrote he was wholly himself; we in our turn must follow him, not by copying his manner, but by being genuinely ourselves.

But I have conceded enough to the time-spirit, and it is on the note of tradition that I want to end. To write good English we must be ourselves: yes, but then we can improve ourselves, else why are we at Cambridge? The best style is the style of the best kind of man, and here in this University there should, if anywhere, be an opportunity of becoming that kind. And this opportunity consists largely in contact with tradition, with the best that has been thought and said in the world. If you seek the kingdom of heaven first, by which I here mean the state of being liberally educated, style will be added to you. Study the great masters, not to imitate them, but to catch something of their spirit; they will help you to be yourself, and at the same time to become a better self. No true originality is ever hampered by such study, for originality means, not having no roots, but having one's own roots, and the richer the soil they draw nourishment from the better. Wise traditionalists, like Sir J. Reynolds, or Matthew Arnold, or 'Q', or Mr Eliot, have never asked us to copy the great models, but to be aware of them, to be ever conscious of the past in the present, and of the present in relation to the past. We in England have always been skilled in adapting the old to new uses, and though our style must be contemporary, it must still be English. Finally, I come back to 'Q's' favourite text: writing is an art, and like every art, it must be practised. Sir Max Beerbohm (in his Rede Lecture three years ago) compared writing with violin-playing. 'We do not say to a violinist', he said (as some say to would-be writers), 'Just think clearly what you want to express and then go ahead. Never mind how you handle your bow.' Think of this analogy constantly, as you write your essays! Practise the literary scales assiduously, and then, when you play your pieces, never be satisfied with the ragged and ill-turned phrase, the broken sentence-structure, the discordant note, the poor intonation, or anything but the most finished performance. 'English must be kept up', as Keats once said, and in striving to keep it up you will be helping to preserve that precious heritage which many of you have risked your lives to defend.

www.ingramcontent.com/pod-product-compliance
Ingram Content Group UK Ltd.
Pitfield, Milton Keynes, MK11 3LW, UK
UKHW020449010325
455719UK00015B/492